THE BLACK GLASS CEILING Breakers

BLACK COWGIRLS & FEMALE PIONEERS OF THE WEST

A STORY WRITTEN BY
DR. NORMA MCLAUCHLIN

Table of Contents

Prologue	3
Introduction	13
Chapter 1: Bridgitt "Biddy" Mason	24
Chapter 2: Susie Summer Revels Carter	34
Chapter 3: Mary Fields	45
Chapter 4: Elizabeth Yhorn Scott Floodk	56
Chapter 5: Abby Fisher	67
Chapter 6: Mary Ellen Pleasant	76
Chapter 7: Cathay Williams	88
Chapter 8: Clara Brown	100
Chapter 9: Aunt Rittie, Henrietta Williams Foster	109
Chapter 10: Johanna July	12
Chapter 11: Jennifer Williams	13
Conclusion	129
Epilogue	130
Appendix	132
	134

Prologue

As the rain poured down outside, Haven found herself once again in her grandmother's attic, a place that had begun to feel like home. This was her second visit, the atmosphere was cozy, with the sound of raindrops tapping against the roof creating a comforting backdrop. The attic, filled with the scent of old books and memories, seemed to beckon her to explore its treasures once more. This time she was drawn to the stories of the cowgirls and black women who were pioneers.

During this visit, Haven had a new sense of purpose. She was eager to delve into the stories of the remarkable women she had read about. Today, she felt an even stronger connection to their journeys, inspired by the resilience and courage they had shown in the face of adversity. She popped open her grandmother's trunk and donned a cowgirl hat and posed in the mirror for a moment before grabbing the book that held the secrets of the stories of cowgirls and pioneers erased from many history books.

One story particularly resonated with her—Jasmine Williams , a young aspiring cowgirl who had just begun her journey in rodeo. Jasmine's story mirrored Haven's own dreams of breaking barriers and finding her place in the world. With each page she turned, Haven could envision Jasmine , a twelve-year-old girl just like her, determined to ride into the future with confidence and hope.

She had been inspired by the women who came before her, including legends like Carmen, Clara, and Stagecoach Mary. She had spent hours practicing her barrel racing and honing her roping skills, eager to leave her mark on the rodeo circuit. She represented the new generation of Black cowgirls, carrying the torch passed down by those who had fought for their place in the sport.

Through her journey, she faced challenges, just as her predecessors had. There were moments of doubt and fear, but she drew strength from the stories of those remarkable women who had paved the way.

She knew that she was not alone in her struggles; the legacy of Black cowgirls was alive and thriving, and she was proud to be a part of it.

As Haven immersed herself in Jasmine's story, she felt a surge of excitement and inspiration. She envisioned herself standing alongside Jasmine ready to take on the world. The attic felt alive with possibilities, and Haven could almost hear the laughter and encouragement of the women who had come before her.

With each word, she felt a deeper connection to her heritage and the rich tapestry of stories woven by Black cowgirls throughout history. "I want to be brave like them," she whispered to herself, her heart swelling with determination. The stories of these women had become her guiding light, illuminating the path ahead.

In her mind, she could see jasmine preparing for her first rodeo competition, surrounded by friends and family who believed in her.

The excitement in the air was palpable as they cheered her on, encouraging her to chase her dreams. "You've got this!" they would shout, their voices ringing with support.

As the day of the competition approached, she faced a mix of nerves and excitement. She practiced tirelessly, envisioning herself racing around the barrels. The night before the event, she shared her fears with her mother. "What if I mess up?" she asked, biting her lip. Her mother smiled and replied, "Just remember, it's not about perfection; it's about having fun and doing your best. And if you fall off, just get back up and laugh about it!"

As the rain continued to fall outside, Haven felt a sense of connection to the legacy of Black cowgirls. She understood that their stories were not just tales of the past; they were a source of inspiration for the future. The attic may have been filled with old memories, but it was also a place of hope and possibility.

With a renewed sense of wonder, Haven looked around the attic, her fingers still tingling from the worn leather journal she had just set down. The rain tapped softly against the roof, but inside, the air buzzed with possibility. Around her, the dust-covered keepsakes and forgotten trunks no longer felt old—they felt alive, like portals to stories waiting to be told. The tale of the Black cowgirl she had just read stirred something deep within her, a fire she couldn't ignore. She knelt beside the chest once more, heart racing with the thrill of discovery. Who else had carved their path across open skies and untamed land? What other secrets did this treasure hold? Haven didn't know yet—but she couldn't wait to find out.

INTRODUCTION

The American West has long been portrayed as a land of adventure, open skies, and rugged cowboys. But beyond the well-worn legends lies a powerful, often overlooked truth: Black women helped shape the West just as boldly—riding horses, running ranches, building towns, and breaking barriers.

Their stories are rich with resilience, bravery, and grit. "They didn't just survive; they thrived," said Dr. Elaine Harper, a cultural anthropologist. These women faced both the harsh realities of frontier life and the deep injustices of racism and sexism—and still, they carved out lives of meaning and legacy.

"You know, it's not just the cowboys who make the West," said historian Sarah Mitchell. "The women—the unsung heroines—are just as crucial to this narrative." For too long, their contributions have been buried beneath myths and silence.

INTRODUCTION

Women like Biddy Mason, who fought in court for her freedom and won. Like Mary Fields, known as "Stagecoach Mary," who fearlessly delivered mail through treacherous terrain. Like Clara Brown, who rose from enslavement to become a beloved businesswoman and philanthropist. These women did not wait for permission to make history—they simply did.

"I had to prove myself time and time again," said modern-day rodeo rider Jennifer Williams, echoing the legacy of those who came before her. Their stories remind us that courage is timeless, and representation matters.

In the pages ahead, you'll discover some of these stories—told through the eyes of a young girl named Haven, who uncovers a hidden trunk in her grandmother's attic. What begins as a simple moment of curiosity becomes a doorway to history, memory, and magic.

Because the legacy of Black cowgirls isn't just history—it's a call to ride forward, boldly and unapologetically.

DEDICATION

For the fearless women who rode against the odds and inspired the next generation of cowgirls. Your legacy lives on in every dream chased and every barrier broken.

Chapter 1

The Groundbreaker
Bridgitt "Biddy" Mason

The attic was quiet, except for the occasional creak of wood and the gentle hum of wind against the roof. Haven sat cross-legged beside the book, her fingers trailing over its worn cover. She hadn't even turned the page this time. The air itself had started to buzz.

Then, a faint sound—the rustle of skirts, the stomp of boots, the clip-clop of hooves on dry dirt—echoed softly from between the pages. A warm, earthy scent filled the air. Lavender, leather, and dust.

The light in the attic dimmed. And once again, the world shifted.

Haven blinked and found herself standing on a dusty trail just outside a small town. The year was somewhere in the mid-1800s—she could tell by the horse-drawn wagons creaking past and the wide skirts swaying in the breeze.

Beside a modest wooden house, a woman knelt in a garden, tending to herbs and flowers with strong, worn hands. Her sleeves were rolled up, and sweat dotted her brow, but her expression was calm—wise, even.

"Excuse me," Haven said gently.

The woman looked up. Her dark eyes sparkled like flint catching sunlight.

"Well now," she said, smiling. "A new face. You don't look like you're from around here."

"I'm not," Haven admitted. "Are you... Biddy Mason?"

"I am," the woman said, standing to her full height, wiping her hands on her apron. "But most folks just call me Biddy."

Biddy led her to a small bench by the garden. As they sat, Biddy began to share her story—not with bitterness, but with strength.

"I was born into slavery back in Georgia, 1818. My hands have always known hard work—plowing fields, raising children, tending the sick. But my mind?" She tapped her temple. "That was always free."

Haven leaned forward. "Did you always want to be free?"

"I always knew I was meant to be," Biddy replied. "But knowing and getting there? That's the hard part."

She told Haven how she'd been taken west by her enslaver, Robert Smith, in 1848. Though California was a free state, Smith tried to keep her and her daughters in bondage.

"I wasn't going to let him," Biddy said, her voice steely. "I found a lawyer, filed a lawsuit, and in 1856—I won. Stood right there in a courtroom and claimed my freedom."

Haven gasped. "You took him to court?"

"And beat him," Biddy said proudly, "with nothing but the truth and a fierce will."

As they walked together through town, Biddy pointed to buildings she'd helped fund—a small church, a schoolhouse, a meeting hall.

"With the money I earned from my laundry business, I bought land. I built places where our people could gather, learn, and grow," she said. "You don't just break chains for yourself—you break them for the ones coming behind you."

They stopped by a corner lot where women hung clothes to dry and children chased chickens through the yard. One little girl looked up and waved.

"You see her?" Biddy said. "That child's future is bigger than anything I could've dreamed. And that's the point. I planted seeds. The harvest? That's for the next generation."

Suddenly, the air shimmered again. The garden, the town, the sun—it all began to fade like watercolor in the rain.

Haven blinked.

She was back in the attic.

The book lay open in her lap, and across the page was a glowing passage:

Biddy Mason was born into slavery in 1818 and later became one of the first Black women to successfully petition for her freedom in California.

She went on to become a landowner, nurse, midwife, and philanthropist—founding churches, supporting schools, and helping build the early Black community in Los Angeles.

She died in 1891, leaving behind a legacy of compassion, leadership, and courage.

At the bottom of the page, one of Biddy's favorite sayings was etched in gold:

"You don't just build a life—you build a legacy."
Haven smiled, her heart full.
And then—just as the last whisper of the West faded from the room—she turned the page.

Comprehension Questions

1 **What significant legal victory did Biddy Mason achieve in California?**
_____
_____
_____
_____
_____

2 **How did Biddy Mason contribute to her community after gaining her freedom?**
_____
_____
_____
_____
_____

Comprehension Questions

3 Discuss the importance of education in Biddy Mason's life and how it influenced her future.
_____
_____
_____
_____

Chapter Activities

LETTER WRITING

Write a letter to Biddy Mason, expressing what her story means to you and how it inspires you to overcome challenges.

_____
_____
_____
_____
_____
_____
_____
_____
_____
_____
_____
_____
_____
_____
_____
_____
_____
_____
_____
_____
_____
_____

Chapter Activities

Create a timeline of Biddy Mason's life, highlighting key events and achievements.

Chapter 2
The Pioneer of Freedom and Community
Susie Summer Revels Carter

The attic was still. Sunlight poured through the dusty window, painting golden streaks across the wooden floor. Haven traced a finger along the spine of the book, still warm from her last journey with Biddy Mason.

She hadn't even whispered a word when a faint sound tickled her ears.

Children laughing.

A fiddle playing.

The sizzle of something delicious on a fire.

Then, in a rush of wind and color, the attic vanished.

Haven stumbled forward onto a sun-baked path, where canvas tents flapped in the breeze, and women in long dresses bustled past carrying baskets of bread and jars of lemonade. Flags fluttered. Music played. The scent of cornbread and roasted peanuts danced through the air.

It was a festival—vibrant, proud, and alive with joy. Standing at the center of it all was a woman in a deep purple dress, her silver-streaked hair tied back neatly, save for a few curls that had escaped, swaying in the breeze like they had minds of their own.

She called out in a voice that rang like a bell: "Let the Summer Revels begin!"

Children rushed forward, some skipping, some tumbling over one another to gather near the stage. Haven stood frozen, until the woman turned and locked eyes with her.

"You there," she said with a grin. "Yes, you with the curious eyes. Come closer. What's your name?"

"Haven," she said softly.

"Well, Haven, I'm Susie Summer Revels Carter—and you've arrived just in time for the parade of possibility."

Later that evening, as the festival wound down, Susie sat with Haven beneath the lantern-lit canopy of a sycamore tree. Laughter echoed from nearby, but the space around them felt sacred.

"I was born in Tennessee," Susie began, stirring the air with her fan. "To parents who had been enslaved. The war ended, and freedom came—but freedom without knowledge? That's no real freedom at all."

Haven nodded, listening closely.

"I studied every letter I could find," Susie continued. "Books were like magic spells. And when I could read... the world opened wide."

She told Haven about her dream to teach other children—Black children—who'd been told they weren't allowed to learn.

"I traveled west, far from home," she said. "Set up a schoolhouse where there was none. Used a potbelly stove to keep warm and chalk from broken limestone to write on old wood. But oh, those children..." Her voice softened. "They lit up like stars."

They walked through a garden of paper lanterns and festival booths as Susie continued to share her passion—not just for education, but for celebration.

"Every year, I host this festival," she said proudly. "It's a place to remember who we are—our music, our stories, our strength. This is how we shine."

Haven watched her interact with families, shaking hands and handing out apples and ribbon-bound books. Her spirit was a mix of joy and purpose, like a warm fire that never went out.

"Did you ever feel like giving up?" Haven asked.

"Of course," Susie replied. "But then I'd look at the children, the women in my town, the seeds I'd planted. And I'd say to myself: 'Susie, you didn't come this far to stop growing now.'"

Suddenly, the sound of fiddles faded. The lanterns dimmed. The air shimmered like heat rising off the earth. Haven blinked—

And she was back in the attic.

The book lay open in her lap, glowing softly. On the page was a tribute written in looping, delicate script:

Though not widely recorded in history books, Susie Summer Revels Carter represents the many Black women educators who transformed their communities in the aftermath of slavery. They opened schoolhouses in barns and basements, organized cultural celebrations, and championed literacy as a form of freedom. Their names may be forgotten—but their work lives on.

At the bottom of the page was her quote:

"Never underestimate the impact of a single teacher."

Haven smiled and whispered, "Thank you, Susie."
And with a heart full of fire and festival dreams —

She turned the page.

Comprehension Questions

1 **What motivated Susie to pursue education, and how did it impact her life?**

_____
_____
_____
_____

2 **In what ways did Susie contribute to her community as an educator?**

_____
_____
_____
_____

Comprehension Questions

3 **Discuss Susie's role in advocating for women's rights and how it shaped her legacy.**

_____

_____

_____

_____

Chapter Activities

Research a modern-day educator who has made a significant impact on their community. Create a presentation comparing their work to Susie's.

Chapter Activities

Essay Prompt

Write a short essay about the importance of education for empowerment, using Susie's life as a reference.

_____
_____
_____
_____
_____
_____
_____
_____
_____
_____
_____
_____
_____
_____
_____
_____
_____
_____
_____
_____
_____
_____

Chapter 3
The Legendary Mail Carrier of the West
Mary Fields

The book practically vibrated in Haven's hands, like it couldn't wait to tell her the next story. She braced herself—just as the page turned itself.

Suddenly, the floor beneath her shook.

RUMBLE. CREAK. WHINNY.

She wasn't in the attic anymore.

She was on the back of a wooden stagecoach, bouncing up and down as the wheels clattered over rocky terrain. Dust swirled all around her, and the air smelled of pine trees, sweat, and adventure.

And up front—gripping the reins like a general commanding her troops—was a towering woman with a long braid and a don't-mess-with-me grin.

"You better hold on tight!" the woman bellowed, cracking the reins. The horses surged forward, and the coach lunged like a rocket.

Haven yelped, grabbing a rail. "Are we—are we going fast enough!?"

The woman turned her head slightly, her eyes glinting. "Child, I am the speed."

As the coach slowed to a halt by a small Montana outpost, the driver tipped her hat and hopped down with surprising grace for someone so sturdy.

"You must be new to the West," she said, offering her hand. "Name's **Mary Fields. Folks call me Stagecoach Mary. And you are?"

"Haven," she breathed, shaking her hand. "I've… heard of you."

Mary chuckled. "Bet you have. Ain't many women lookin' like me, doin' what I do."

She stood nearly six feet tall, with skin darkened from the sun and arms strong enough to lift a horse. Her boots were dust-covered, and her long skirt swayed like she didn't have time for nonsense.

Haven followed her through the camp, past men tipping their hats in respect and kids running up to hug her legs.

"You always this popular?" Haven asked.

Mary winked. "Only on Tuesdays. And Thursdays. And Sundays."

They sat by a campfire as the sun dipped below the horizon, casting golden light across the plains. Mary took a sip of coffee and looked out at the hills.

"I was born a slave in 1832, down South. Got my freedom after the war. Worked hard. Real hard. Cooked, cleaned, hauled freight. But it wasn't until I came out West that I could breathe."

She stared into the fire, her voice deep but steady. "I took a job as a stagecoach driver for the U.S. Postal Service—first Black woman to do it. Some folks thought I couldn't handle it." She laughed. "They were wrong."

Haven leaned closer. "Were you ever scared?"

Mary's eyes softened. "Scared? Sure. Bandits, blizzards, busted wheels. But you don't let fear drive your wagon. You drive it."

Later, Mary showed Haven her horses, brushing their manes and whispering to them like old friends.

"They listen to me 'cause I listen to them," she said, handing Haven a brush. "Gentle strokes. That's it."

"You really did all this by yourself?" Haven asked.

Mary shrugged. "Nobody does it by themselves. I had friends. I had faith. And I had these beauties." She patted the horse's neck. "People said I didn't belong behind the reins. So I gripped 'em tighter."

As the stars bloomed above them and the fire crackled low, Haven felt the world begin to shimmer again.

Mary smiled knowingly. "Don't forget what I told you, sugar. You don't wait for permission to make your mark. You ride for it."

Haven opened her mouth to reply, but—

SWOOSH.

She was back in the attic.

The book lay open, its pages glowing in soft gold. On the paper, new words had appeared, almost as if written by Mary herself:

Mary Fields, known as Stagecoach Mary, was the first African American woman to carry mail for the U.S. Postal Service.

She protected her route with a rifle and a fearless spirit, braving snowstorms, wild animals, and discrimination in the rugged terrain of Montana.

She became a beloved community member, known for her generosity, her strength, and her refusal to back down.

And beneath that, her words, like an echo from the trail:

"I lived my life on my own terms."

Haven closed her eyes and whispered, "And what a life it was."

Then she reached for the next page—

And held on tight.

Comprehension Questions

1 **What challenges did Mary Fields face as a woman in a male-dominated profession?**

_____

_____

_____

_____

2 **Describe Mary Fields' contributions to her community beyond her work as a stagecoach driver.**

_____

_____

_____

_____

Comprehension Questions

3 How did Mary Fields' love for horses influence her life and career?

_____

_____

_____

_____

Chapter Activities

Create a visual representation (poster or infographic) of Mary Fields life, highlighting her achievements and community contributions.

Chapter Activities

Writing Prompt

Write a fictional diary entry from Mary Fields' perspective on a day in her life as a stagecoach driver.

_____
_____
_____
_____
_____
_____
_____
_____
_____
_____
_____
_____
_____
_____
_____
_____
_____
_____
_____
_____
_____
_____
_____
_____

Chapter 4
Forging Community and Breaking Barriers
Elizabeth Thorn Scott Flood

The attic was silent, save for the soft rustling of pages as Haven opened the book to its next chapter. A gentle breeze stirred, carrying with it the faint scent of chalk and aged paper. Suddenly, the world around her shifted.

Haven found herself standing in front of a modest wooden house in Sacramento, California. The year was 1854. Children of various ages gathered eagerly outside, their eyes filled with anticipation. A woman with a warm smile and determined eyes stood at the doorway, welcoming each child with open arms.

"Come in, everyone," she called. "Today, we embark on a journey of knowledge."

Haven approached the woman, who turned to her with a curious glance.

"Hello there," the woman said kindly. "I'm Elizabeth Thorn Scott Flood. And you are?"

"I'm Haven," she replied. "It's an honor to meet you."

Inside, the room was simple but filled with the spirit of learning. Desks were arranged neatly, and a blackboard stood at the front. Elizabeth addressed the class with enthusiasm.

"Education is the key to our future," she declared. "No matter the obstacles, we will learn and grow together."

After the lesson, Elizabeth shared her story with Haven. Born free in New York in 1828, she had moved to California during the Gold Rush with her husband, Joseph Scott. After his untimely death, she faced the challenge of educating her son in a society that denied Black children access to public schools. Undeterred, she established a private school in her home, welcoming not only Black children but also Native American and Asian American students.

As they walked through the neighborhood, Elizabeth spoke of her dreams.

"I envision a world where every child, regardless of race, has the opportunity to learn," she said. "We must build that world together."

Haven felt inspired by Elizabeth's unwavering commitment to education and equality.

The scene began to fade, and Haven found herself back in the attic, the book resting in her lap.

On the open page, words glowed softly:

Elizabeth Thorn Scott Flood (1828–1867) was a trailblazing educator who established the first private school for Black children in Sacramento, California.

Her efforts laid the foundation for desegregated education in the state, and she is remembered as a pioneer in the fight for equal educational opportunities.

At the bottom of the page, a quote stood out:

"Education is the key to our future."

Haven smiled, her heart filled with admiration for the woman who had turned her home into a beacon of hope.

Who Was Elizabeth Thorn Scott Flood?
- Born: 1828 in New York (some sources list 1829)
- Died: 1867
- Known For: Being one of the first African American women to establish a school for Black children in California

Major Accomplishments

- Founded the First School for Black Children in Sacramento
  - In 1854, after discovering that her son was not allowed to attend the public schools in Sacramento due to segregation, Elizabeth opened a private school for African American children in her own home.
  - This school was the first of its kind in Sacramento, offering education to children who would otherwise be denied it.
- Advocated for Equal Education
  - She strongly believed in the power of education as a tool for liberation and worked tirelessly to improve educational opportunities for children of color.
  - Later, she also worked with Native American and Asian American children, creating one of the earliest multiracial learning spaces in California.
- Paved the Way for Desegregation
  - Her work laid the foundation for the eventual desegregation of California schools and helped establish the importance of early childhood education for marginalized communities.

Comprehension Questions

1 **What challenges did Elizabeth Thorn Scott Flood face as a Black woman trying to start a school in California during the 1850s?**

_____
_____
_____

THINK ABOUT THE LAWS AND ATTITUDES TOWARD RACE AND EDUCATION DURING THAT TIME.

2 **Why was it important that Elizabeth opened her own school, and how did it help her community?**

_____
_____
_____
_____

Comprehension Questions

3 Elizabeth believed education could lead to freedom and change. What are some ways she made a difference in the lives of others?

_____

_____

_____

_____

CAN YOU THINK OF A WAY HER WORK STILL MATTERS TODAY?

Career Exploration

Conduct a mock business pitch for a business idea inspired by Elizabeth's entrepreneurial spirit.

Chapter Activities

Writing Prompt

Write a poem celebrating Elizabeth Yhorn Scott Flood's resilience and contributions to society.

_____
_____
_____
_____
_____
_____
_____
_____
_____
_____
_____
_____
_____
_____
_____
_____
_____
_____
_____
_____
_____

Chapter 5
A Trailblazer in Barre Racing
Abby Fisher

The attic smelled of cinnamon and aged paper. Haven stood still for a moment, her fingertips grazing the edge of a worn page. She didn't need to turn it—this time, the book turned itself. The golden edges shimmered, the attic blurred, and suddenly, the air grew thick with the scent of nutmeg, fried cornmeal, and slow-simmered greens.

WHOOSH!

A swirl of flour sparkled like fairy dust, and Haven blinked as her sneakers landed—plop—on the creaky wooden floor of a busy 1800s kitchen in San Francisco. Cast iron pots clanked, the air buzzed with voices, and the comforting warmth of a bustling stove wrapped around her like a hug.

"Child, you best not stand in the doorway unless you're helpin' or tastin'!" a deep, melodic voice called from the center of the whirlwind.
Haven turned to see her: tall, dignified, with flour-dusted fingers and kind eyes that twinkled behind thick lashes. Her apron read Mrs. Abby Fisher & Co., Pickles, Preserves & Southern Delights.

"You—you're Abby Fisher!" Haven gasped.

Abby chuckled, wiping her hands on her apron. "I reckon I am. And you're not from around here, are you?"

Haven spent the day by Abby's side, learning the rhythm of a kitchen led by heart and memory. Abby moved like she was dancing, stirring with one hand while giving instructions with the other. "Cooking ain't just about feeding folks," she said, lifting a bubbling pot to Haven's nose. "It's how we remember. How we honor who we are."

"Did you always want to cook?" Haven asked, watching her fold biscuit dough with precision.

"I was born into slavery in South Carolina," Abby said, her voice quieting. "I couldn't read or write, but I could taste, mix, and measure like nobody else. After the war set us free, I made my way out West, where I turned what I knew into something no one could take away."

Haven watched in awe as Abby handed her a worn recipe card—dictated, not written, since Abby had never learned to read.

Yet her cookbook, What Mrs. Fisher Knows About Old Southern Cooking, would go on to become one of the first published by a Black woman in the United States.

Later that evening, Abby stood before a small gathering of neighbors and friends in her kitchen, proudly holding up a glass jar of preserves. "This here is more than jam," she told them. "This is our story, sealed and sweet. I may not know letters, but I know flavor, and I know love."

Cheers erupted, and someone passed Haven a plate of golden cornbread dripping with honey.

"I never knew food could be a kind of history," Haven whispered to Abby.

Abby winked. "Everything has a story, child. Even a spoonful of stew."

As the kitchen faded and the attic's cool air returned, Haven found herself back on the floor with the book open on her lap. The final lines of the page shimmered in soft golden ink:

Abby Fisher (c.1831–c.1915) rose from slavery to become a celebrated chef, businesswoman, and one of the first African American women to publish a cookbook. Though she couldn't read or write, she dictated over 160 recipes that preserved generations of culinary heritage in her book What Mrs. Fisher Knows About Old Southern Cooking, published in 1881.

Beneath it, a quote sparkled like a signature: **"Our food tells our story."** — **Abby Fisher**

Haven wiped her hands on her jeans, still able to smell the cornbread.

"On to the next chapter," she whispered, her heart as full as her belly.

Comprehension Questions

1 What was Abby Fisher's most notable achievement in the culinary world?

_____
_____
_____

2 How did Abby overcome the challenges she faced as a Black woman in the culinary industry?

_____
_____
_____
_____

Comprehension Questions

3 Discuss the significance of Abby's cookbook and its impact on Black culinary traditions.

_____

_____

_____

Chapter Activities

Create a recipe inspired by Abby Fisher's Southern cuisine and share it with the class. Pick something truly delicious!

NAME OF DISH:

Ingredients:

-
-
-
-
-
-
-

DIRECTIONS:

SPACE FOR NOTE:

Chapter Activities

Writing Prompt

Write a review of Abby's cookbook as if it were published today, discussing its relevance and importance.

Chapter 6
Secrets of a Golden City
Mary Ellen Pleasant

The attic was quiet, save for the ticking of Granddad's old clock. Haven ran her fingers along the cracked leather binding of the next journal. The gold lettering shimmered under the light: "Mary Ellen Pleasant: The Millionaire Who Fought in Silence."

She had barely opened the first page when the floor beneath her gave a gentle rumble. The scent of bay water and iron filled the air. A whoosh of wind curled around her ankles.

Haven's heart fluttered. "Here we go again…"

With a flash of gold and a blink, the attic melted away—and she found herself standing on a cobbled street in 1850s San Francisco.

The city buzzed with energy. Ships lined the harbor, men shouted about gold, and women in bonnets bustled past in horse-drawn carriages. But it wasn't the glitter of gold that pulled Haven's eyes—it was the tall Black woman standing confidently on the porch of a fine house.

She wore a pressed gown with lace cuffs, and a pearl pin nestled in the collar of her blouse. Her eyes scanned the street like she saw through it.
"That's her," Haven whispered. "Mary Ellen Pleasant."

"Come in, child. You look like you've seen a ghost," Mary Ellen said with a smile as she opened the door.
Haven blinked. "I—I think I traveled here somehow."

Mary Ellen chuckled softly, leading her through polished mahogany halls into a sunlit sitting room. "Well, San Francisco has seen stranger things."
They sat over tea, steam curling like whispers in the air. Through the window, the city moved, unaware that one of its most powerful women was quietly changing history.

"I've worn many masks," Mary Ellen said, pouring tea with grace. "Cook, servant, investor... abolitionist."

"Weren't you scared?" Haven asked.

"All the time," Mary Ellen replied. "But I learned that power often lives where people least expect to find it. And I used that surprise to my advantage."

Mary Ellen took Haven to one of her boarding houses behind the bustling docks.

"These walls hide more than rest," she said. "They're stops on the Underground Railroad. People come here on their way to freedom."

She showed Haven ledgers written in invisible ink, documents with fake names, and a thick envelope.

Inside was a check—$30,000 to John Brown, the famed abolitionist preparing for revolt.

"You funded a rebellion?" Haven gasped.
Mary Ellen nodded. "Quietly. Powerfully. Not all revolutions need a war cry."

On their walk back, Mary Ellen and Haven boarded a streetcar. The conductor stared at them.

"No coloreds," he barked.

Mary Ellen didn't flinch. "Then you'll have to remove me yourself."

The car jolted forward. No one dared move her. Later, Mary Ellen leaned close to Haven. "I'll sue them. And I'll win. You don't always need fists to fight—you just need to know the law better than they do."

The wind shifted again. The street blurred. Haven felt that tug in her chest—the familiar pull of time letting go.
"Thank you," she whispered. "For everything."
Mary Ellen Pleasant pressed a small folded note into her hand. "Remember this: Silence does not mean surrender. Sometimes it's the sound of strategy."

With a shimmer and a swirl, Haven was gone.

Back in the attic the book lay open, a fresh sentence etched across the page:

She fought with finance, with law, with silence—and won more battles than history could count.

Haven tucked the note from Mary Ellen inside the journal and smiled. Another ceiling broken. Another truth reclaimed.

5 FASCINATING FACTS ABOUT MARY ELLEN PLEASANT

1. SHE SECRETLY FUNDED ABOLITIONIST JOHN BROWN
MARY ELLEN GAVE $30,000 TO SUPPORT HIS PLAN TO END SLAVERY—MAKING HER A QUIET FORCE BEHIND ONE OF HISTORY'S BOLDEST ACTS OF RESISTANCE.

2. SHE HELPED DESEGREGATE SAN FRANCISCO STREETCAR
AFTER BEING FORCED OFF A STREETCAR, SHE SUED THE COMPANY—AND WON—HELPING TO END SEGREGATION IN CALIFORNIA'S PUBLIC TRANSPORTATION IN 1868.

3. SHE WAS A CONDUCTOR ON THE UNDERGROUND RAILROAD
BEFORE MOVING WEST, SHE HELPED ENSLAVED PEOPLE ESCAPE TO FREEDOM USING HIDDEN NETWORKS AND DISGUISES.

4. SHE USED HER ROLE AS A SERVANT TO GAIN POWER
WORKING IN ELITE HOMES, SHE COLLECTED VALUABLE INFORMATION AND BUILT INFLUENTIAL CONNECTIONS—ALL WHILE FURTHERING ABOLITIONIST EFFORTS.

5. HER GRAVESTONE HONORS HER ACTIVISM
THOUGH HISTORY TRIED TO ERASE HER, HER HEADSTONE PROUDLY STATES: "SHE WAS A FRIEND OF JOHN BROWN."

Comprehension Questions

1 How did Mary Ellen Pleasant use her wealth and social position to support the fight against slavery?

_____

_____

_____

2 What risks did Mary Ellen Pleasant take when she challenged segregation in San Francisco's streetcar system?

_____

_____

_____

Comprehension Questions

3 Why do you think Mary Ellen Pleasant's contributions to civil rights were overlooked for so long, and how is her legacy being honored today?

_____

_____

_____

_____

_____

_____

_____

Chapter Activities

- Debate the effectiveness of Mary Ellen Pleasant's strategies in advocating for civil rights.
- Create a visual timeline of significant events in Mary Ellen Pleasant's life, focusing on her contributions to social justice.

Chapter Activities

Writing Prompt

Write a reflective essay on the impact of community leaders like Mary Ellen Pleasant on society.

_____
_____
_____
_____
_____
_____
_____
_____
_____
_____
_____
_____
_____
_____
_____
_____
_____
_____
_____
_____

Chapter 8
Angel of the Rockies
Clara Brown

A quiet moment had settled over the attic, golden light filtering through the window like soft honey. Haven sat cross-legged on the floor, still catching her breath from her last journey. Her fingers gently brushed the edge of the next page, but this time, she didn't turn it right away. Something about the stillness felt sacred—like the silence before a song begins.

She reached out slowly. The paper felt warm under her fingertips.

Whoosh.

The room spun. Dust and rafters melted away. Suddenly, the scent of pine trees filled her nose, mixed with wood smoke and fresh-baked bread. Haven blinked against the bright sunlight—only to realize she was no longer in the attic.

She was standing in the middle of a bustling mining town in the Colorado mountains. Wooden buildings framed a dirt road, and everywhere she looked, people hurried by in boots and bonnets, baskets of laundry on their hips or pickaxes slung over their shoulders.

A tall Black woman with kind eyes and streaks of silver in her hair bustled past, balancing a steaming tray of cornbread and stew. "Come on in now, don't be shy!" she called to the crowd. Her voice was warm and powerful—like a hymn wrapped in honey.

Haven's heart skipped.

"Clara Brown," she whispered.

The woman turned, as if she'd heard.

"Well now, who are you, baby?" Clara asked, tilting her head with a smile.

"I—I'm Haven," she stammered. "I'm… just visiting."

Clara chuckled. "Well then, Haven-the-visitor, come lend a hand. Folks need feeding, and I've got stew that won't stir itself."

Before she could blink, Haven found herself inside a large wooden house that smelled of cinnamon, soap, and sunshine. Clara's home bustled with children, travelers, even miners with muddy boots. Clara moved through the room with grace, checking on a sick boy in the corner, folding clean laundry, and greeting each person like family.

"Everyone calls me Aunt Clara," she explained, handing Haven a basket of biscuits. "This place is more than a house—it's a refuge. A place for folks who lost everything... like I once did."

They sat together later that night beside a crackling fire. Clara's hands, wrinkled and strong, folded neatly in her lap.

"I was born into slavery in Virginia," she began, voice low. "Married young. Had four children. But when my owner died, they sold us all off like cattle. I lost every one of them."

Haven's chest tightened. "I'm so sorry," she whispered.

Clara nodded slowly. "It nearly broke me. But I held on to faith—and when I was freed at 56, I left Kentucky and joined a wagon train west. Cooked for 26 men just to get to Denver. Folks weren't thrilled about a Black woman on the trail, but I kept my head high."

She smiled. "When I reached the mountains, I started a laundry. Then a bakery. Then bought land and mines. People said it couldn't be done—but baby, I did it."

Haven's eyes widened. "That's incredible!"

"I used what I had to help others. Sent for freed folks back in Kentucky. Gave to churches. Hosted the first Sunday school in my home. My daughter... I searched for her for years. And when I was 82—" her voice caught, tears bright in her eyes, "I found her."

They sat in silence, the crackle of fire wrapping around them like a lullaby.

"I wasn't born with riches," Clara said softly, "but I died rich in love. That's what matters."

The firelight faded, the mountain air cooled, and the world began to blur. Haven was back in the attic. But something had changed.

She looked down at the open book. New words glowed on the page, facts gently unfolding before her eyes:

Clara Brown was the first Black woman to settle in Colorado. She invested in businesses and mines, helped over 16 formerly enslaved

people start new lives, and was honored by state leaders at her funeral. They called her the Angel of the Rockies.

Haven pressed a hand to her heart.

"She really was."

5 KEY FACTS ABOUT CLARA BOWN

1. SHE WAS BORN INTO SLAVERY IN 1800
CLARA BROWN WAS BORN ENSLAVED IN VIRGINIA AND LATER LIVED IN KENTUCKY. AFTER BEING GRANTED HER FREEDOM AT AGE 56, SHE WAS REQUIRED BY LAW TO LEAVE THE STATE OF KENTUCKY.

2. SHE WAS ONE OF COLORADO'S FIRST BLACK SETTLERS
CLARA TRAVELED WEST ON A WAGON TRAIN IN 1859 AND BECAME THE FIRST RECORDED AFRICAN AMERICAN WOMAN TO SETTLE IN COLORADO DURING THE GOLD RUSH ERA.

3. SHE BUILT A SUCCESSFUL BUSINESS EMPIRE
CLARA WORKED AS A LAUNDRESS, MIDWIFE, COOK, AND NURSEMAID. SHE EVENTUALLY OWNED PROPERTY AND MINING CLAIMS ACROSS COLORADO—INCLUDING 16 LOTS IN DENVER AND 7 HOUSES IN CENTRAL CITY—ACCUMULATING OVER $10,000 (A SIGNIFICANT FORTUNE AT THE TIME).

4. SHE HELPED RESETTLE MORE THAN 16 FORMERLY ENSLAVED INDIVIDUALS
AFTER THE CIVIL WAR, CLARA USED HER WEALTH TO HELP FREED BLACK FAMILIES MOVE TO COLORADO, PROVIDING THEM WITH HOUSING, JOBS, AND A SUPPORTIVE COMMUNITY.

5. SHE WAS HONORED AS A COLORADO PIONEER
IN HER LATER YEARS, CLARA WAS INDUCTED INTO THE SOCIETY OF COLORADO PIONEERS AND WAS POSTHUMOUSLY INDUCTED INTO BOTH THE COLORADO WOMEN'S HALL OF FAME (1989) AND THE COLORADO BUSINESS HALL OF FAME (2022).

Comprehension Questions

1 What obstacles did Clara Brown face after gaining her freedom?

_____
_____
_____
_____

2 How did Clara contribute to her community in Colorado?

_____
_____
_____
_____

Comprehension Questions

3 Discuss the significance of Clara Brown's legacy in the context of empowerment and resilience.
_____
_____
_____
_____

Chapter Activities

Create a community service project inspired by Clara Brown's dedication to helping others.

Chapter Activities

Writing Prompt

Write a short story imagining Clara Brown's life if she lived in today's world.

Chapter 9

Aunt Rittie rides at dawn

Aunt Rittie, Henrietta Williams Foster

The attic was still, but the air around Haven shimmered like heat rising off a desert trail. She reached for the book again—this time, its cover seemed warmer, almost pulsing. As she opened to the next chapter, a gust of wind burst through the tiny attic window, flipping the pages wildly until they stopped on their own.
Suddenly, the scent of sagebrush and saddle leather filled her nose.

In the blink of an eye, Haven was no longer standing on the creaky attic floor—she was atop a dusty ranch trail in South Texas. The sun was just rising, casting gold across the prairie, and a figure on horseback was approaching fast. A white horse galloped closer, hooves thudding like a heartbeat. Riding sidesaddle in a long faded skirt, with eyes sharp as flint and a braid trailing down her back, came a woman like none Haven had ever seen.

"Well, you just gonna stand there and squint, or are you coming with me?" the woman called out, pulling her horse to a stop with ease. "Name's Rittie. Aunt Rittie to most."

Haven scrambled to climb onto a nearby fencepost. "I—uh—I've never ridden a horse before."

Aunt Rittie gave a low chuckle. "Then it's a good day to learn."

As they rode, Aunt Rittie showed Haven the life of a cowhand—branding cattle, roping strays, riding bareback across the open land. "Don't think being a woman means I can't outwork a man," she said, handing Haven a rope. "Out here, respect is earned with grit, not gossip."

Haven noticed the butcher knife Aunt Rittie kept tucked in her waistband. "Is that... for protection?"

Rittie smirked. "Only if someone's foolish enough to need reminding that I ain't one to mess with."

They stopped by a grove where Rittie pointed out wild herbs growing beneath a twisted oak tree. "This here's yarrow—good for cuts. And that's red raspberry leaf—helps a woman stay strong." She spoke gently, her fingers brushing each leaf with reverence. "I've brought babies into this world, healed fevers, and stood up to men who thought I shouldn't be here at all."

By the time the sun reached its peak, Haven's shirt was damp with sweat, but her heart was soaring. She'd never met anyone like Aunt Rittie—bold, fearless, and full of quiet wisdom. They sat under the tree with the horses tethered nearby as Aunt Rittie poured water from a canteen.

"You know," she said, "I never learned to read or write. But I knew how to work. And I knew how to live free—even when the world didn't want me to."

The wind kicked up again, swirling dust around them. As Haven blinked, the prairie faded, and she was back in the attic. The book lay open at her feet, the pages now glowing faintly.
She picked it up and read:

Henrietta "Aunt Rittie" Williams Foster was born into slavery in 1827 and became a legendary cowhand in South Texas. She worked ranches, rode horses, served as a midwife, and healed with herbal knowledge passed down through generations. She demanded respect.

She defied expectations, leaving behind a legacy of strength, skill, and independence—one ride at a time.

Haven pressed a hand to her heart. "Aunt Rittie," she whispered. "You rode through history like a storm."

And with that, she looked to the next page, ready for wherever the story would take her next.

3 LITTLE KNOWN FACTS ABOUT 'AUNT RITTIE'

1. SHE ALWAYS CARRIED A BUTCHER KNIFE
AUNT RITTIE WASN'T JUST TOUGH—SHE WAS LEGENDARY. KNOWN FOR KEEPING A BUTCHER KNIFE ON HER AT ALL TIMES, SHE USED IT NOT JUST FOR WORK BUT ALSO AS A SYMBOL OF HER INDEPENDENCE AND WILLINGNESS TO DEFEND HERSELF IN A MALE-DOMINATED, OFTEN DANGEROUS FRONTIER.

2. SHE WAS A SELF-TAUGHT HERBALIST AND HEALER
THOUGH SHE NEVER LEARNED TO READ OR WRITE, AUNT RITTIE BECAME A SKILLED MIDWIFE AND HEALER. SHE USED HERBS AND NATURAL REMEDIES, PASSED DOWN THROUGH ORAL TRADITION, TO TREAT INJURIES AND ILLNESSES ON THE RANCH AND IN NEARBY COMMUNITIES. HER HEALING HANDS WERE TRUSTED BY MANY ACROSS TEXAS—BLACK, WHITE, AND INDIGENOUS ALIKE.

3. SHE OUTSMARTED RANCH OWNERS AND COWBOYS
AUNT RITTIE, KNOWN FOR HER UNMATCHED HORSEMANSHIP, CATTLE-WRANGLING SKILLS, AND QUICK WIT, EARNED RESPECT—ON SOUTH TEXAS RANCHES TYPICALLY DOMINATED BY WHITE MEN. COWBOYS WHO UNDERESTIMATED HER QUICKLY LEARNED A LESSON WHEN SHE BEAT THEM AT THEIR OWN GAME.

Comprehension Questions

1 What role did Aunt Nellie play in her community?

_____
_____
_____
_____

2 How did her experiences as a formerly enslaved woman shape her commitment to helping others?

_____
_____
_____
_____
_____

Comprehension Questions

3 **How did Aunt Rittie's skills and presence challenge stereotypes about Black women in the Old West?**

_____
_____
_____
_____
_____
_____
_____
_____
_____
_____

Chapter Activities

Activity: Create Your Own Wild West Persona

1. **Learn the Era:**
   Briefly research life in the American West for Black pioneers like Aunt Rittie.

2. **Build a Character:**
   Create a frontier persona with:
   - A name and nickname
   - Special skill (e.g., riding, roping, healing)
   - A personal challenge
   - A short "tall tale" moment

3. **Tell the Story:**
   Write a journal entry or perform a short monologue as your character.

Bonus:
   Design a fun "Honor Poster" with fun facts and a sketch of your character.

Chapter Activities

Writing Prompt

Aunt Nellie defied the odds as a Black woman cowboy in the American West, earning respect in a field dominated by white men. In a well-organized essay, explore how her courage, skill, and determination helped her break barriers. What lessons can we learn from her story about facing challenges and redefining what's possible?

Chapter 10
Wild Horses, Brave Heart
Johanna July

The attic air was warm with summer wind, fluttering the edges of the old book as Haven reached for it. But this time, before her hands could touch the page, the spine cracked open on its own, glowing with golden light. The scent of dust and leather gave way to sun-scorched prairie and river mist. Suddenly, Haven was standing knee-deep in the Rio Grande.

Across the water, a tall woman with long, braided hair sat astride a wild horse, guiding it through the current with skillful ease. Her dress, spun in vivid homespun colors, clung to her like a badge of pride, and a necklace of gold beads danced with each movement. "You here to learn how we tame more than just horses out here?" the woman called, her voice rich like the Texas soil. "Name's Johanna July. Most folks just call me Chona."

Haven blinked in awe. "You broke that horse—in the river?"

Johanna grinned. "Best way to gentle the wild ones. Water humbles them, teaches respect.

Same with people sometimes." With a practiced move, she swung her leg and slid off the horse, water dripping from her skirts. "Come on. Let's see what you're made of."

Over the next few days, Haven watched Johanna at work—herding goats, commanding horses, and holding her own in a world not built for women like her. Cowboys would scoff until Johanna out-rode, out-wrangled, and out-witted them. She had inherited her father's land and legacy, and she ran it with the grit of a dozen men. "They don't expect someone like me," she told Haven one evening by the fire. "Black. Seminole. Woman. But I don't ride for their expectations. I ride for my own name."

Haven nodded, soaking in every word. Johanna taught her how to balance on a bareback pony, how to read the wind before it changed, and how to see strength in being underestimated. And when it was time to go, Johanna placed a smooth river stone in Haven's palm. "Take it back with you. Remember—your story's got power too."

Back in the attic, Haven sat cross-legged, holding the warm stone. She read the final lines of Johanna's chapter:

Johanna July, born around 1860 in Nacimiento, Mexico, became one of the most skilled horsebreakers of the American West. A Black Seminole woman, she trained horses for the U.S. Army, ran a ranching business, and defied every barrier in her path. Her legacy gallops on as a symbol of strength, freedom, and the fierce spirit of the frontier.

Haven smiled, heart pounding like hooves across the open plains. There was more to learn, more to discover. But for now, she whispered, "Thank you, Chona," and gently closed the book.

> "I didn't break horses to prove anything—I did it because freedom has always run wild in my blood."
>
> Johanna July

Comprehension Questions

1 What challenges did Johanna July face as a Black Seminole woman breaking horses in the American West?

_____

_____

_____

_____

2 How did Johanna use her skills to support and protect her community?

_____

_____

_____

_____

Comprehension Questions

3 In what ways did Johanna July defy the expectations of women during her time?
_____
_____
_____
_____
_____

4 What is your favorite fact about this character and why?
_____
_____
_____
_____
_____

Chapter Activities

Writing Prompt

Write a personal reflection on how Johanna's story inspires you to pursue your passions and advocate for others.

Chapter Activities

Host a discussion panel with peers about the importance of representation in various fields, using Johanna July as an example.

Chapter 11
One Final Ride
Jennifer Williams

Haven didn't mean to fall asleep in the attic, but the dusty afternoon light was so soft and warm, she must've dozed off with the book in her lap. When she blinked awake, the pages were fluttering—turning on their own—as if the book still had one more story to tell. A familiar voice whispered through the breeze.

"Time for one last ride," Grandma said, stepping into the attic with a knowing smile.
Before Haven could answer, the room filled with the scent of leather saddles and sun-warmed hay. The attic vanished, replaced by the hum of an arena crowd, the creak of boots on wooden planks, and the rhythmic thud of hooves hitting dirt.

They were backstage at a modern rodeo, where a woman stood tall in jeans and a denim shirt, clipboard in hand and determination in her eyes.
"That's Jennifer Williams," Grandma whispered. "You might not always see her in the spotlight, but she's the reason the lights shine for others."

Haven watched as Jennifer checked ropes, gave last-minute pep talks, and adjusted her daughter Hali's helmet before a big run. "You've got this, baby girl," she said, her voice filled with calm strength. Her husband, Speed Williams, was nearby, focused and intense—but it was Jennifer who grounded the whole family, managing their rodeo legacy with grace, grit, and deep love.

"She's not just a mom or a wife," Grandma added. "She's the backbone of champions."

Haven learned that Jennifer had supported her husband through eight world championships and guided her daughter Hali into her own record-breaking career in breakaway roping. She wasn't competing—but she was coaching, organizing, praying, planning, and holding everything together behind the scenes. Her belief in her family never wavered. She gave them the wings to fly.

"Every rider needs a solid ground crew," Jennifer said, crouching to tie a young rider's boot. "Success in this world comes from family, faith, and fierce love."

The arena faded, and the attic returned. The book was closed now, resting in Haven's hands like it knew the journey was over. She looked up at Grandma, eyes wide.

"Was she a pioneer too?" Haven asked.

Grandma nodded. "In her own way. Not every trailblazer rides out front. Some build the trail itself."

And with that, Haven knew—the story wasn't just about cowgirls, or even about history. It was about love passed down through generations. About holding tight to your dreams, and the people who help you chase them.

The attic grew quiet as the last shimmer of rodeo dust faded into the air. Haven blinked and looked around—back home again. The sun was setting outside the window, casting a golden hue over the wooden floorboards and the open book that now sat still in her lap. Her heart was full—not just with stories, but with strength, legacy, and purpose.

Grandma placed a gentle hand on Haven's shoulder. "You've seen what most history books leave out," she said, her voice warm with knowing. "Black cowgirls, trailblazers, pioneers—they may not have made the headlines, and many of their stories were lost or left behind. But they were always there, shaping the land, shaping our legacy. Their strength carved out space for us to stand tall, even in places that weren't built to welcome us. They broke barriers with quiet courage and powerful love. And now, baby girl, their fire burns in you."

Haven nodded, her eyes shining with new understanding. She looked at the book one last time, then gently closed it—like tucking away a sacred secret. The attic air felt still, but inside her, everything had changed. Maybe it was wisdom. Maybe it was pride. Or maybe it was the unshakable truth that in every forgotten chapter, there were women like her—bold, brilliant, and brave—riding forward into history.

She stood slowly, taking Grandma's hand. "I won't forget them," she whispered.

Grandma smiled, eyes gleaming. "Good. Because one day, someone just might open a book... and find you."

Comprehension Questions

1 What challenges does Jennifer Williams face as a modern-day cowgirl?

_____
_____
_____
_____

2 How does Jennifer use her platform to inspire and empower others?

_____
_____
_____
_____

Comprehension Questions

3 Discuss the significance of Jennifer's adequacy for inclusivity in the rodeo and ranching communities.

_____
_____
_____
_____
_____
_____

Chapter Activities

Writing Prompt

Write a creative piece (story, poem, or song) that reflects the themes of empowerment and resilience in Jennifer's journey.

_____
_____
_____
_____
_____
_____
_____
_____
_____
_____
_____
_____
_____
_____
_____
_____
_____
_____
_____
_____

Community Performance

Create a social media campaign that promotes the stories of underrepresented figures in the cowboy community, inspired by Jennifer Williams.

Conclusion

The stories of Black cowgirls and women of the American West illuminate the resilience, strength, and pioneering spirit of those who defied societal norms and overcame adversity. "We are the architects of our future," one might hear at community gatherings, a sentiment echoed by many of the women whose stories have been shared. From Biddy Mason's legal triumphs to Jennifer Williams' modern-day advocacy, these women have made significant contributions to their communities and the broader fabric of American history. Their legacies serve as powerful reminders of the importance of representation, empowerment, and the relentless pursuit of dreams.

By sharing these narratives, we honor their journeys and inspire future generations to continue breaking barriers and striving for equality. "Let us carry their stories forward," a community leader might say, encouraging everyone to remember the strength of those who came before. These women remind us that every voice matters and that every story contributes to the rich tapestry of our collective history.

Activity Ideas

1. Reflective Essay: Write a reflective essay on how the stories of these women have influenced your understanding of resilience and empowerment. What lessons can you apply to your own life?

2. Group Discussion: Organize a group discussion where students can share their thoughts on the common themes found in the stories of these women. How do their experiences relate to current societal issues?

3. Create a Legacy Project: Design a project that honors one of the women discussed in the chapters. This could be a community event, a digital presentation, or a written pie that celebrates her contributions.

Vocabulary

1. **Resilience:** The ability to recover quickly from difficulties; toughness.

2. **Advocate:** A person who publicly supports or recommends a particular cause or policy.

3. **Entrepreneur:** A person who organizes and operates a business, taking on financial risks to do so.

4. **Philanthropy:** The desire to promote the welfare of others, expressed especially by the donation of money to good causes.

5. **Empowerment:** The process of becoming stronger and more confident, especially in controlling one's life and claiming one's rights.

6. **Representation:** The action of speaking or acting on behalf of someone or the state of being represented.

7. **Legacy:** Something handed down by a predecessor; an amount of money or property left to someone in a will.

APPENDIX

This appendix includes additional resources and materials related to the themes and individuals discussed in the book. It provides readers with opportunities for further exploration and understanding of the impact of Black women in the American West.

1. **Suggested Reading:**
   - Black Women of the Old West by William Loren Katz
   - African American Women of the Old West by Tricia Martineau Wagner
   - A Black Woman's West: The Life of Rose B. Gordon by Bruce A. Glasrud
   - She Came to Slay: The Life and Times of Harriet Tubman by Erica Armstrong Dunbar
   - Sweet Taste of Liberty: A True Story of Slavery and Restitution in America by W. Caleb McDaniel
   - Ida: A Sword Among Lions by Paula J. Giddings

Appendix Contd.

2. **Online Resources:** Websites and digital archives where readers can find primary sources, photographs, and additional stories related to the topics covered in this book:

- Schomburg Center for Research in Black Culture:

https://www.nypl.org/locations/schomburg

- National Museum of African American History and Culture:

https://nmaahc.si.edu

- BlackPast.org (African American history, biographies, primary documents):

https://www.blackpast.org

- Library of Congress – African American History Collections:

https://www.loc.gov/collections

- Women & the American Story (New-York Historical Society):

https://wams.nyhistory.org

Appendix Contd.

3. **Organizations:** Websites and digital archives where readers can find primary sources, photographs, and additional stories related to the topics covered in this book:

- Association of Black Women Historians (ABWH):

https://www.abwh.org

- National Coalition of 100 Black Women:

https://ncbw.org

- Black Girls Do Ride (Celebrating Black women equestrians and cowgirls):

https://blackgirlsdoride.com

- African American Museum of Dallas:

https://aamdallas.org

- Zinn Education Project – Teaching people's history:

https://www.zinnedproject.org

REFERENCES

1. Mason, Biddy. "The Life of Biddy Mason: A Pioneer in the American West." Edited by John Smith, Historical Publishing, 2020.

2. Carter, Susie Summer Revels. "Educating the Future: The Life and Legacy of Susie Summer Revels Carter." By Maria Thompson, Education Press, 2019.

3. Fields, Mary. "Stagecoach Mary: The Life and Times of Mary Fields." By Sarah Johnson, Western Historical Society, 2021

4. Flood, Elizabeth Yhorn Scott. "Breaking Barriers: The Entrepreneurial Spirit of Elizabeth Yhorn Scott Flood." By Patricia Davis, Business History Review, 2018.

5. Fisher, Abby. "The Culinary Legacy of Abby Fisher: Recipes and Reflections." By Emily Carter, Gastronomy Press, 2022.

6. Pleasant, Mary Ellen. "Mary Ellen Pleasant: Advocate for Freedom and Equality." By Rachel Adams, Civil Rights Chronicles, 2017.

REFERENCES CONTD.

7. Williams, Cathay. "A Soldier's Story: The Life of Cathay Williams." By James Robinson, Military History Publications, 2020.

8. Brown, Clara. "Clara Brown: A Legacy of Hope and Resilience." By Angela Smith, Colorado History Press, 2019.

9. Brown, Henietta Aunt Nellie "Aunt Nellie: The Heart of Community Service." By Linda Davis, Community Voices Publishing, 2021.

10. Foster, Ritt Williams. "Women in Business: The Trailblazers of the West." By Karen Lee, Entrepreneurial Women Press, 2020.

11. July, Johanna. "The Modern Cowgirl: Advancing the Legacy of Women in the West." By Zoe Anderson, Contemporary Western Press, 2022.

12. Williams, Jennifer. "Breaking Barriers: The New Generation of Cowgirls." By Michelle Brown, Cowgirl Chronicles, 2023.

www.ingramcontent.com/pod-product-compliance
Lightning Source LLC
Chambersburg PA
CBHW042308150426
43198CB00001B/9